BIRDS

DESERT ANIMALS

Lynn M. Stone

Rourke Publications, Inc.
Vero Beach, Florida 32964

Edited by Pamela J.P. Schroeder

PHOTO CREDITS
Photos p. 15, 18 © Joe McDonald; p. 8 © Steve Bentsen; all other
photos © Lynn M. Stone

ACKNOWLEDGEMENT
The author thanks the staff of the Arizona-Sonora Desert Museum,
Tucson, for its cooperation with some of the photography in
this book.

Library of Congress Cataloging-in-Publication Data
Stone, Lynn M.
    Birds / by Lynn Stone.
        p. cm. — (Desert animals)
    Summary: Describes how birds living in the desert adapt to the
harsh environment.
    ISBN 0-86625-629-6
    1. Birds—Juvenile literature. 2. Desert animals—Juvenile
literature. [1. Birds. 2. Desert animals.] I. Title.
II. Series: Stone, Lynn M.   Desert animals.
QL676.2.S76   1997b
598—dc21   97-16383
                                              CIP
                                              AC

Printed in the USA

TABLE OF CONTENTS

BIRDS

Deserts are dry, and plants are scattered. America's deserts are not wastelands, though. Hundreds of **species** (SPEE sheez), or kinds, of birds visit the deserts.

For many birds, the desert is a rest stop during spring and fall flights to other places.

Dozens of bird species, though, spend their whole lives in the desert. Most of them eat live **prey** (PRAY)—insects, spiders, or small animals. Without much water to drink, eating other animals is one way that desert birds get water.

The mockingbird is one of the many songbirds at home in desert country. The mockingbird's variety of songs is second to none.

CACTUS WREN

The cactus wren is not a visitor to the desert. This wren, the largest of the wrens, spends its life in desert country. It is one of the desert birds that human visitors are most likely to see.

The cactus wren makes several purselike nests of twigs, grass, and other tidbits. Its nests are usually built among the spiny arms of cholla (KOY ya) cactus.

The cactus wren uses one nest to raise a family. The others are for shelter in bad weather.

A cactus wren steps outside of its nest in a spiny cholla cactus. Despite their thorny homes, cactus wrens are rarely speared by spines.

ROADRUNNER

Roadrunners are common desert birds. Their fairly large size—up to 22 inches (56 centimeters)—and curious behavior are not easily missed.

The roadrunner builds its nest above ground, in a shrub or cactus. However, it makes a living on the ground, where it chases and kills scorpions, lizards, and snakes. Sometimes a roadrunner's eyes are bigger than its stomach. Part of its snake or lizard meal may be left dangling from its mouth.

Roadrunners, common in the desert, are members of the cuckoo family. They dash after lizards and snakes.

GAMBEL'S QUAIL

Flocks of Gambel's quail are common in America's desert country. Quail are plump, chickenlike birds.

Quail are not related to roadrunners, but they spend most of their time on the ground, too. Quail are among the few desert birds that live mostly on a diet of plants. They eat foods such as mistletoe berries, cactus fruit, and red tomatillos (toh mah TEEL yohz).

The Gambel's quail is the most handsome desert quail. It wears a feather **plume** (PLOOM), called a topknot, on its head.

A Gambel's quail hustles across a dry streambed in the Sonoran Desert of Arizona. These handsome quail wear feather topknots.

11

Gila woodpeckers are common in the giant saguaro cactus deserts of Arizona and Mexico.

The desert great-horned owl is largest of the desert's nighttime predators on wings.

ELF OWL

The elf owl is the smallest owl in the world. It's an owl of the great saguaro (seh WAHR eh) cactus "forests" in Arizona and western Mexico. The elf owl spends its days in a cactus nest hole. It begins to hunt at **dusk** (DUSK), when the sun goes down.

Because it's just 5 inches (13 cm) long, the elf owl is not a mighty hunter, or **predator** (PRED uh tor). It eats mostly insect prey.

The largest of the desert owls is the great-horned owl.

The little elf owl lives in the southwestern deserts of the United States and Mexico.

HOODED ORIOLE

Not all desert birds are brown or gray. The hooded oriole is one of the most colorful. The male wears beautiful black-and-yellow feathers.

Like most desert songbirds, the hooded oriole eats insects. It catches them with a bill that's more curved than bills of other orioles.

The hooded oriole is a desert visitor in the United States. Each fall it flies south from the American Southwest into warmer country in Mexico.

The hooded oriole male's flashy colors brighten the desert in spring.

HUMMINGBIRDS

Hummingbirds are the smallest of all North American birds. Hummers are only about 3 inches (7.7 cm) long.

Hummingbirds look like flying jewels in the desert sunshine. They feed on insects and the **nectar** (NEK ter) of bright flowers. They reach nectar by dipping their long bills into blossoms. Hummers feed in flight, their wings a blur, like bumblebees.

Several hummingbird species **migrate** (MY grate) through the Southwest as they travel to nesting, or winter, homes. The Costa's hummingbird is a common nesting hummer in desert country.

Hummingbirds in flight sip nectar from desert plants. Bright flowers, especially red ones, attract these tiny birds.

PYRRHULOXIA

The pyrrhuloxia (peer uh LAHK see uh) is a Southwestern cousin of the cardinal. It's about the same size as a cardinal, and it has the cardinal's crest. It even sings like a cardinal! It looks, though, like a cardinal that is spray-painted gray.

Pyrrhuloxias are among the many insect-eating songbirds of the desert. They live in southern Arizona, southeast New Mexico, and southwest Texas. They are more common in Mexico.

The pyrrhuloxia is a southwestern cousin of the northern cardinal. Cardinals also live in desert country.

GILA WOODPECKER

The desert seems an odd place for woodpeckers, but the flicker, ladder-backed woodpecker, and gila woodpecker make the desert home.

The gila woodpecker of the Sonoran Desert in Arizona lives in giant saguaro cactus. The huge saguaro are as large as trees.

The woodpecker hammers out a nest hole in the cactus. At mealtime, it drums insects from the saguaro.

Gila woodpeckers also eat mistletoe berries and cactus fruit.

Glossary

dusk (DUSK) — the period of last light after sunset and before darkness

migrate (MY grate) — to make a long journey at the same time and to the same place each year

nectar (NEK ter) — a sweet liquid made by some flowers

plume (PLOOM) — a long, thin, showy feather

predator (PRED uh tor) — an animal that kills other animals for food

prey (PRAY) — an animal that is killed by another animal for food

species (SPEE sheez) — a certain kind of animal within a closely-related group of animals; for example, a *gila* woodpecker

INDEX

$15.93

DATE			